SKYLANDERS UNIVERSE™

LEARN TO DRAW

GROSSET & DUNLAP
Published by the Penguin Group
Penguin Group (USA) LLC, 375 Hudson Street, New York, New York 10014, USA

USA | Canada | UK | Ireland | Australia | New Zealand | India | South Africa | China

penguin.com
A Penguin Random House Company

© 2015 Activision Publishing, Inc. SKYLANDERS UNIVERSE is a trademark and ACTIVISION is a registered trademark of Activision Publishing, Inc. Published by Grosset & Dunlap, a division of Penguin Young Readers Group, 345 Hudson Street, New York, New York 10014. GROSSET & DUNLAP is a trademark of Penguin Group (USA) LLC. Manufactured in China.

This book was produced by Walter Foster Publishing, a division of Quarto Publishing Group USA Inc.

ISBN 978-0-448-48722-9   10 9 8 7 6 5 4 3 2 1

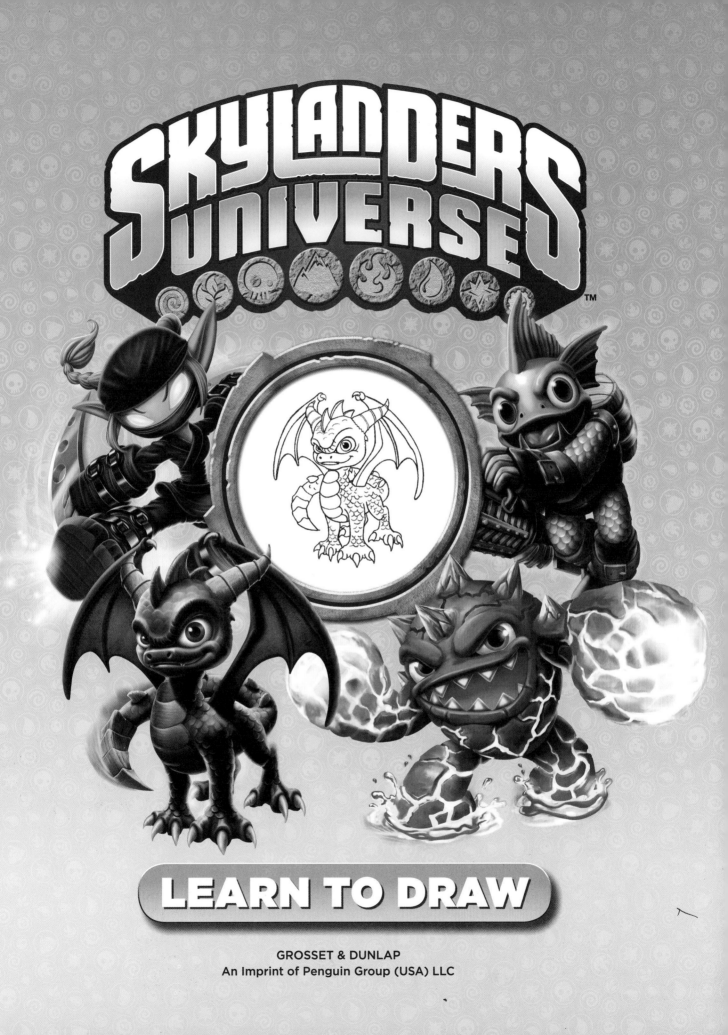

SKYLANDERS UNIVERSE ™

LEARN TO DRAW

GROSSET & DUNLAP
An Imprint of Penguin Group (USA) LLC

For generations, the Skylanders have used their powers and weapons to protect Skylands—a magical world of wonder and adventure that exists between the fabric of the universe.

This infinite expanse of clouds and sky is populated with countless numbers of floating islands where almost anything is possible, but evil also has a presence.

Wise beings called Portal Masters were charged with protecting Skylands. They used magical Portals to look into other regions of Skylands, and even other worlds, to seek out true heroes that they could lead into battle to defend Skylands from danger. The last great Portal Master was Master Eon, who recruited the bravest collection of Skylanders—each with magical powers that align with one of the ten elements (Air, Water, Fire, Earth, Life, Undead, Tech, Magic, Light, and Dark)—in the fight against the evil Kaos!

Using this book, you'll learn to draw your favorite Skylanders. So grab a pencil and start illustrating your own epic adventure in Skylands!

TABLE OF CONTENTS

TOOLS & MATERIALS

Before you begin drawing, you will need to gather a few tools. Start with a regular pencil, an eraser, and a pencil sharpener. When you're finished with your drawing, you can bring your characters to life by adding color with crayons, colored pencils, markers, or even watercolor or acrylic paints!

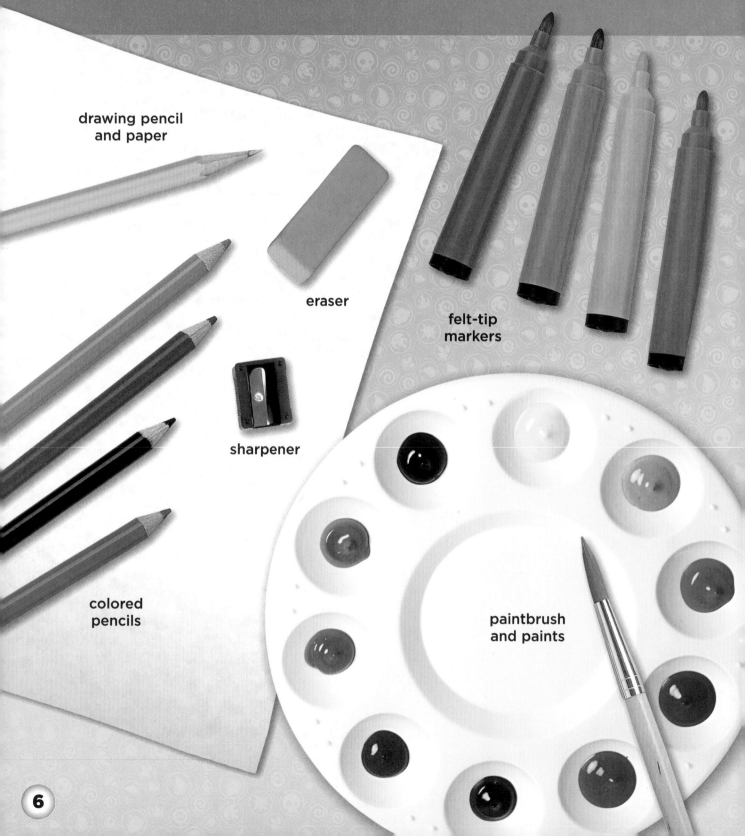

drawing pencil
and paper

eraser

felt-tip
markers

sharpener

colored
pencils

paintbrush
and paints

HOW TO USE THIS BOOK

The first thing you'll need is a pencil with a good eraser. Lots of times when artists draw characters, they make extra lines to help them figure out where to put things like noses and ears and wings. If you use a pencil, you can erase these lines when your drawing is finished.

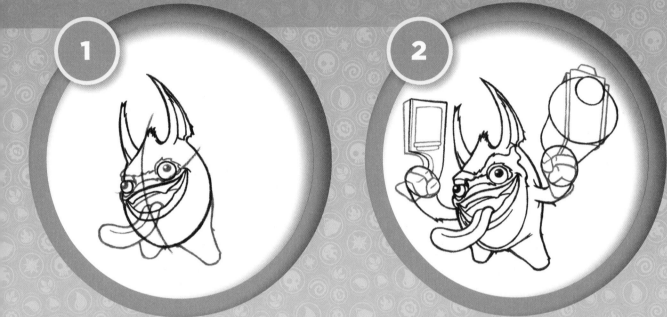

1

Draw the basic shape of the character, then add simple guidelines to help you place the features.

2

Each new step is shown in blue. Simply follow the blue lines to add the details. It will take several steps to add them all.

3

When you finish adding all the details, you can erase your guidelines. Then you can darken your final sketch lines with a pen or a marker.

Add color to your drawing with colored pencils, markers, paints, or crayons.

SPYRO

Spyro hails from a rare line of magical purple dragons that come from a faraway land few have ever visited. It's been said that the Scrolls of the Ancients mention Spyro prominently—the old Portal Masters have chronicled many of his exciting adventures and heroic deeds. Finally, Master Eon himself reached out and invited him to join the Skylanders. From then on, evil faced a new enemy—and the Skylanders gained a valuable ally.

ALL FIRED UP!

POP FIZZ

Nobody is quite sure what Pop Fizz was before he became an alchemist, least of all Pop Fizz himself. After many years of experimenting with magical potions, his appearance has changed quite significantly. In fact, no one even knows his original color. But it's widely known that he is a little crazy, his experiments are reckless, and the accidents they cause are too numerous to measure. Understandably, he has had a difficult time finding lab partners—or anyone that even wants to be near him. In hopes of making himself more appealing to others, he attempted to create the most effective charm potion ever—but that just turned him into a big, wild berserker. Or maybe that's just how he saw the potion working in the first place.

MOTION OF THE POTION!

GILL GRUNT

Gill Grunt was a brave soul who joined the Gillman military in search of adventure. While journeying through a misty lagoon in the clouds, he met an enchanting mermaid. He vowed to return to her after his tour of duty. Keeping his promise, he came back to the lagoon years later, only to learn a nasty band of pirates had kidnapped the mermaid. Heartbroken, Gill Grunt began searching for her all over Skylands. Though he has yet to find her, he joined the Skylanders to help protect others from such evil. He still keeps an ever-watchful eye out for the beautiful mermaid and the pirates who took her.

FEAR THE FISH!

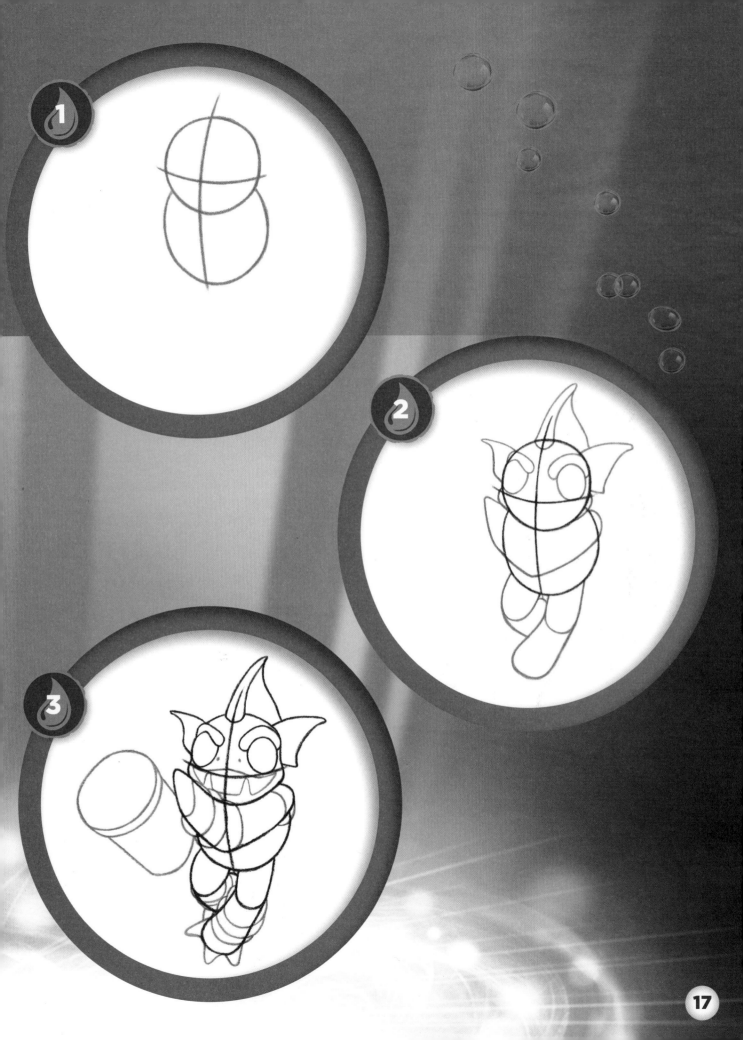

JET-VAC

Jet-Vac was the greatest, most daring flying ace in all of Windham. He was given magical wings when he was young, as was the tradition for all Sky Barons. But when his homeland was raided, he chose to sacrifice his wings to a young mother so she could fly her children to safety. This act of nobility caught the attention of Master Eon, who sought out the young Sky Baron and presented him with a gift—a powerful vacuum device that would allow him to soar through the skies once again. Jet-Vac accepted the gift with gratitude, and now he daringly fights evil alongside the other Skylanders.

HAWK AND AWE!

STEALTH ELF

As a small child, Stealth Elf awoke one morning inside the hollow of an old tree with no memory of how she got there. She was taken in by an unusually stealthy, ninja-like creature in the deep forest. Under his tutelage, she spent the majority of her life learning the art of stealth fighting. After completing her training, she became a Skylander and set out to uncover the mystery behind her origins.

SILENT BUT DEADLY!

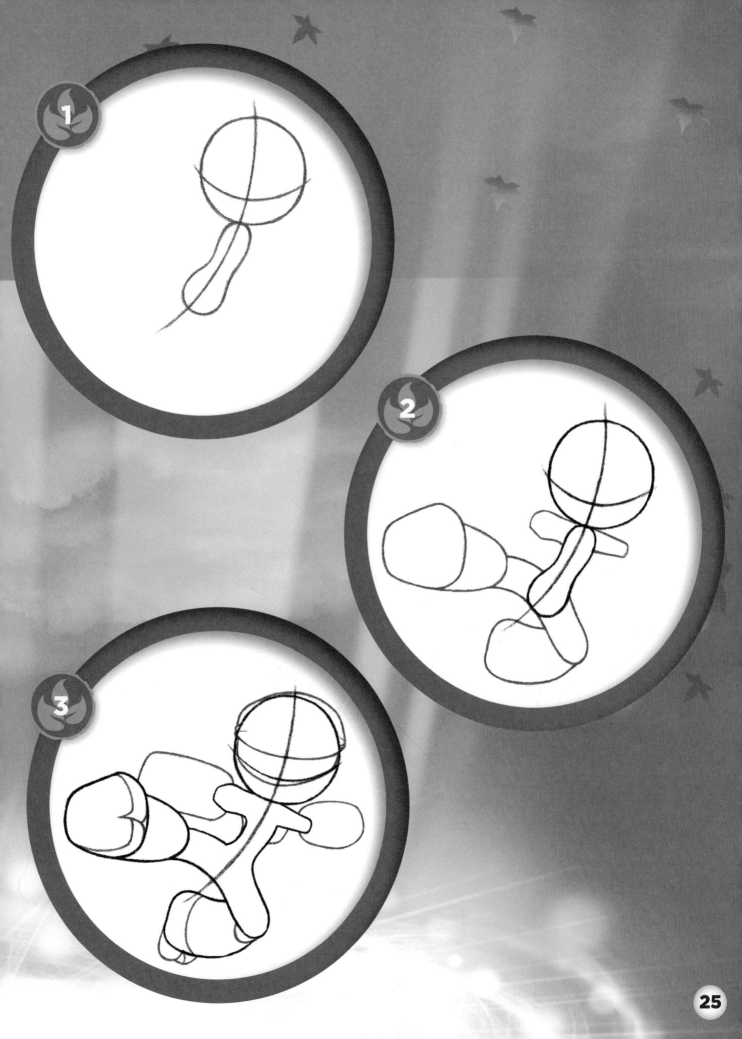

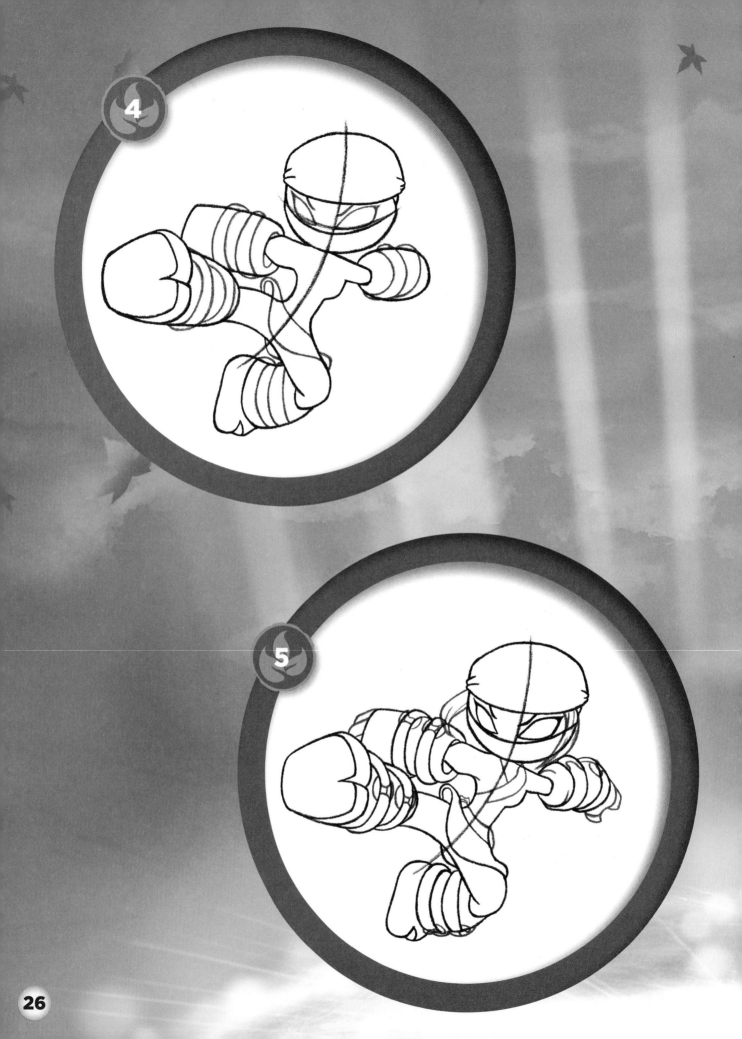

FOOD FIGHT

Food Fight does more than just play with his food—he battles with it! This tough little Veggie Warrior is the byproduct of a troll experiment gone wrong. When the Troll Farmers Guild attempted to fertilize their soil with gunpowder, they got more than a super snack—they got an all-out Food Fight! Rising from the ground, he led the neighborhood Garden Patrol to victory. Later, he went on to defend his garden home against a rogue army of gnomes after they attempted to wrap the Asparagus people in bacon! His courage caught the eye of Master Eon, who decided that this was one veggie lover he needed on his side as a valued member of the Skylanders. When it comes to Food Fight, it's all you can eat for evil!

EAT THIS!

ERUPTOR

Eruptor is a force of nature. He hails from a species that lived deep under a floating volcanic island until a massive eruption launched their entire civilization to the surface. He's a complete hothead—steaming, fuming, and quite literally erupting over almost anything. To help control his temper, he likes to relax in lava pools, particularly because there are no crowds.

BORN TO BURN!

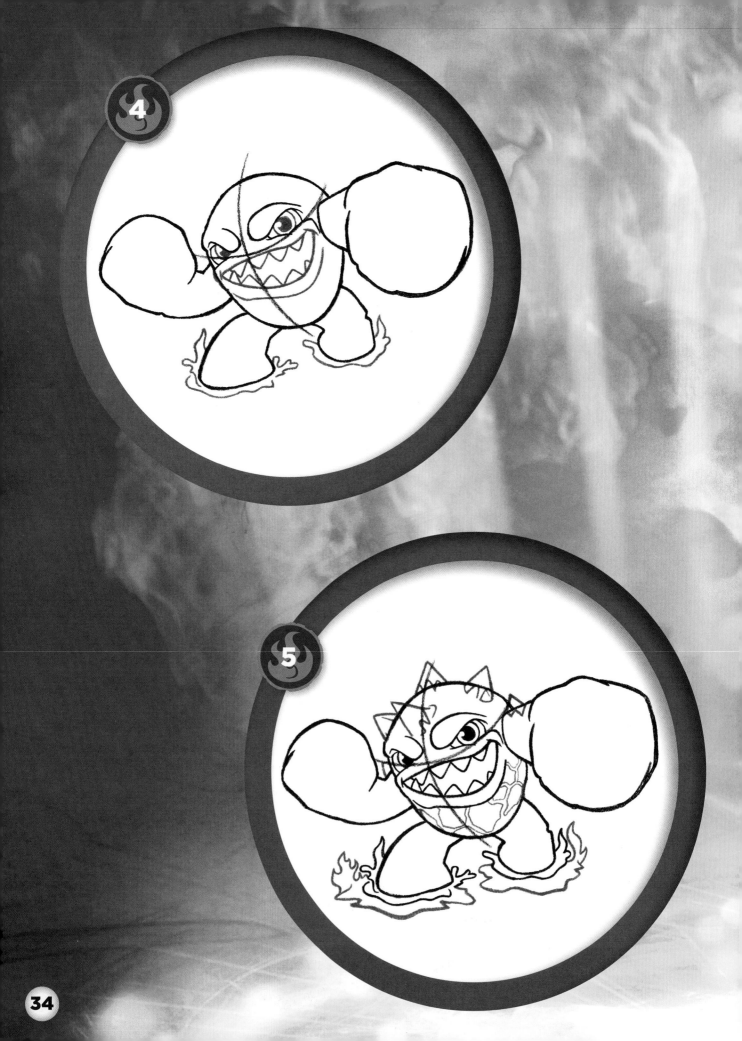

TRIGGER HAPPY

Trigger Happy is more than his name—it's his solution to every problem. Nobody knows where he came from. He just showed up one day in a small village, saving it from a group of terrorizing bandits by blasting gold coins everywhere with his custom-crafted shooters. Similar tales were soon heard from other villages, and his legend quickly grew. Now everyone in Skylands knows of the crazy gold-slinger that will take down any bad guy... usually without bothering to aim.

NO GOLD, NO GLORY!

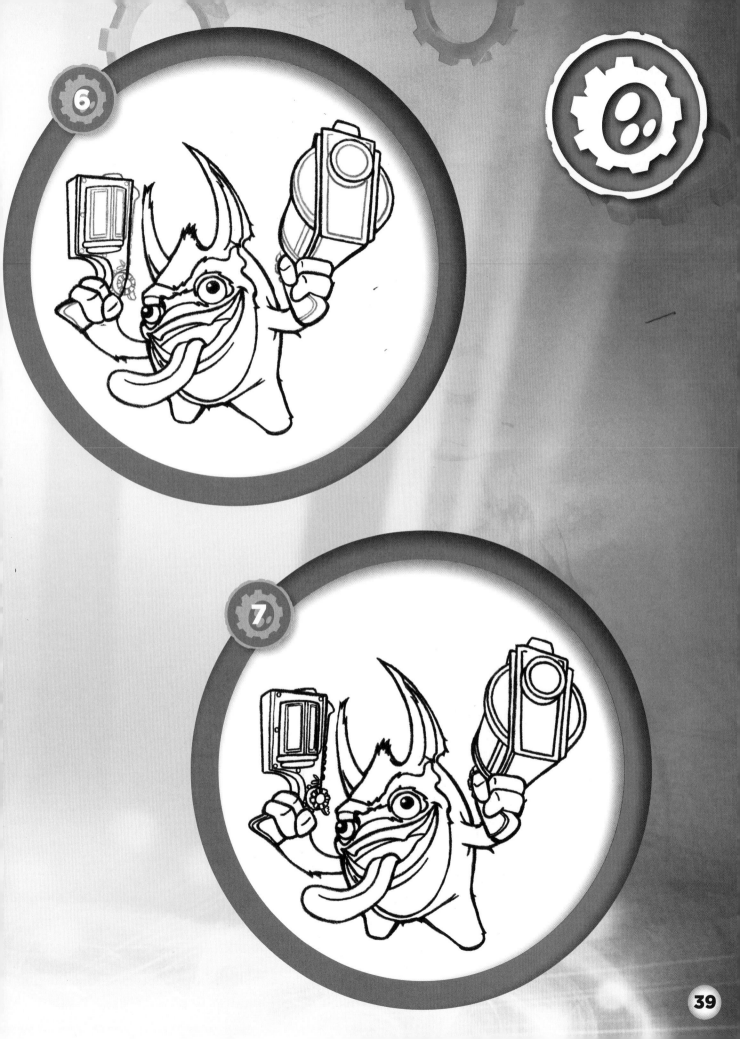

CHOPPER

Growing up, Chopper was much smaller than the rest of his dinosaur kin. But that didn't bother him, because he had big ideas. Ahead of an annual hunting competition held in honor of the village idol, Roarke Tunga, Chopper spent weeks building himself a super Gyro-Dino-Exo-Suit. When the competition began, he took to the air, firing missiles and chomping everything in his path. With Chopper on the verge of victory, the competition came to a sudden halt when a nearby volcano erupted, flooding the village with lava. Seeing the villagers trapped, Chopper quickly flew into action. One at a time, he airlifted everyone to safety. And was even able to save the village idol. For heroically using his head, Chopper was made a Skylander!

DINO MIGHT!

PRISM BREAK

Prism Break was once a fearsome rock golem who didn't like to be disturbed. Then an accidental cave-in left him buried underground. One hundred years later, a mining expedition digging for valuable jewels discovered him by chance with a well-placed blow from a pickax—something Prism Break doesn't talk about. After one hundred years of solitude, he found that the pressure of the earth had transformed him emotionally as well as physically, turning his crude rocky arms into incredible gems with powerful energy. Grateful for being free of his earthly prison, Prism Break decided to put his new abilities to good use and dedicated himself to protecting Skylands.

THE BEAM IS SUPREME!

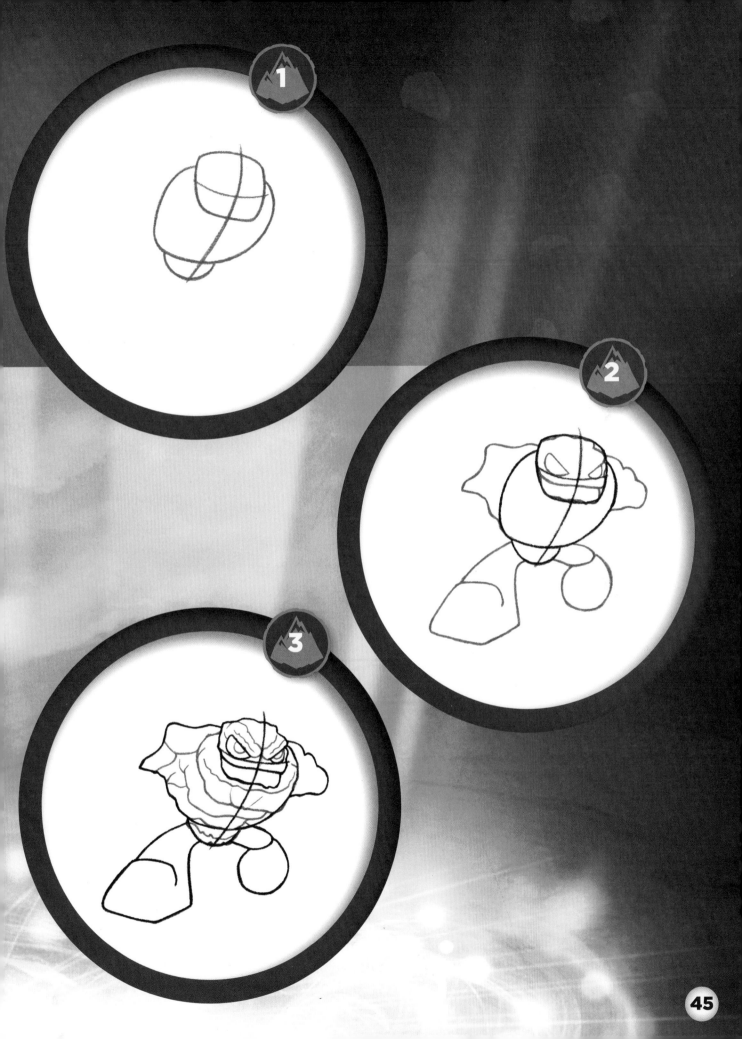

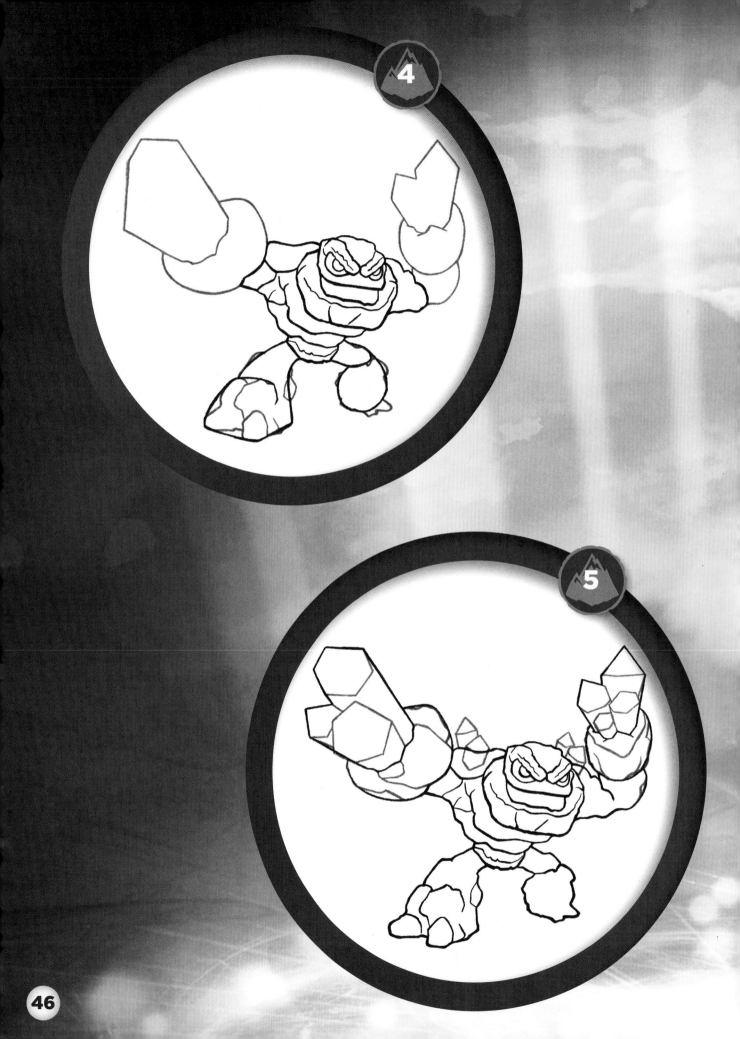

FLASHWING

Flashwing's true origins are a mystery. But her first known appearance came when Bash made a wish that he could fly and looked up to see a shooting star streak across the sky and land in a valley below. In the center of the glowing impact crater was a large, brilliant geode—which suddenly cracked open to reveal Flashwing. Bash may not have soared that day, but his heart sure did, because Flashwing was beautiful . . . and lethal. As soon as Bash stepped closer, the gem dragon turned toward him. Not knowing if he was friend or foe, she blasted him off the cliff with a full-force laser pulse from her tail! Perhaps Bash flew that day after all.

BLINDED BY THE LIGHT!

☠ CHOP CHOP

Chop Chop was once an elite warrior created by the ancient Arkeyans. Like many of the Arkeyans' inventions, he was created from a hybrid of elements—in his case, Undead magic and Tech. Chop Chop is a relentless, highly skilled soldier who wields a sword and shield made of an indestructible metal. After the Arkeyans vanished long ago, Chop Chop wandered Skylands for centuries. Eventually, he was found by Eon and recruited as a Skylander.

SLICE AND DICE!

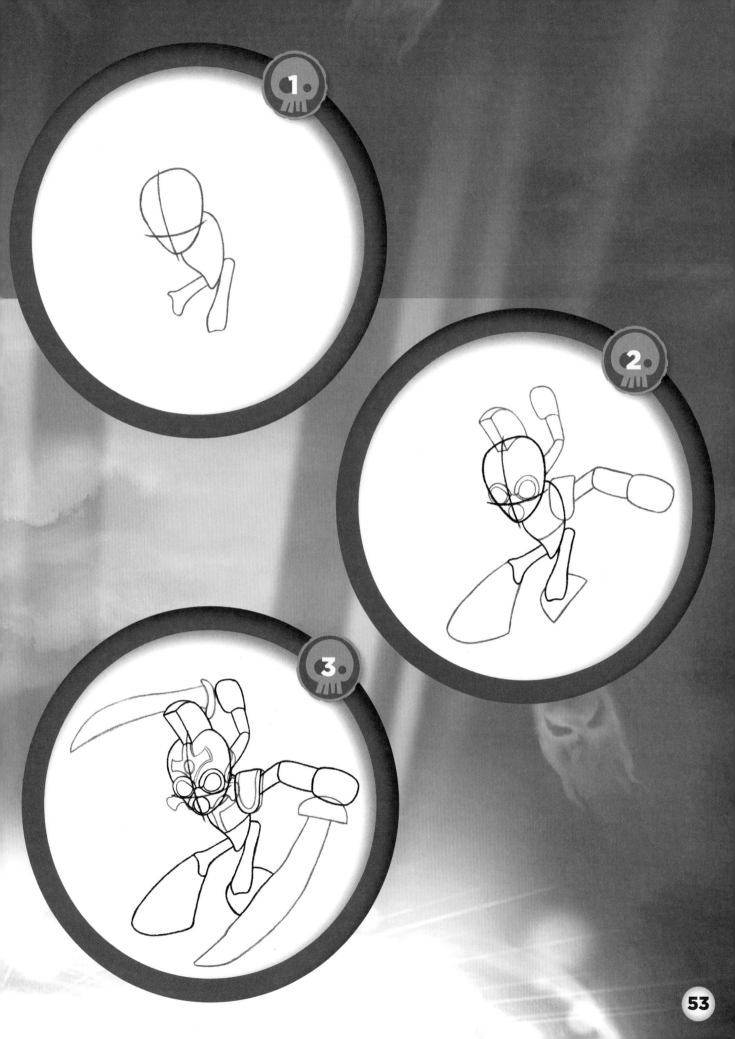

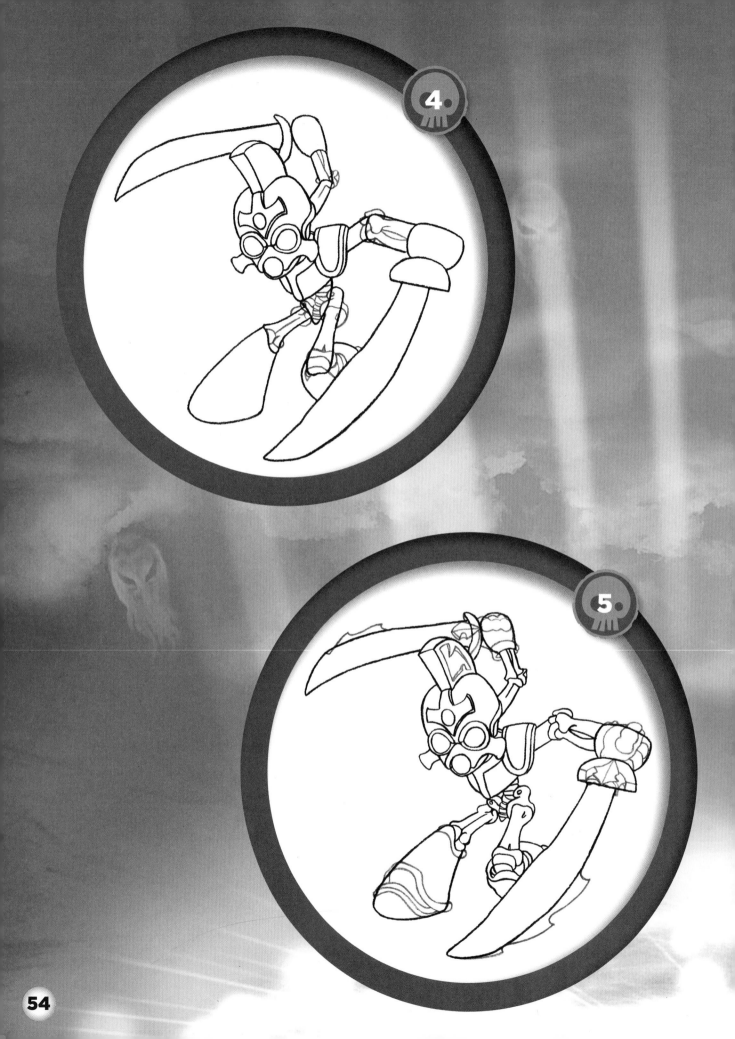

FUNNY BONE

Funny Bone once lived on Punch Line Island, the funniest place in the land of the Undead and home of the Eternal Chuckling Trees that magically make everyone laugh when a breeze tickles them. After hearing stories about the trees, the evil Count Moneybone sent his minions to investigate if this magic could be used to make a Funny Bomb that would render Skylands helpless with laughter. Funny Bone was in the middle of burying his neighbors' birthday cake on a breezeless day when the invaders arrived. Seeing their large axes, Funny Bone instantly knew that the Chuckling Trees were in danger. Without hesitation, he sprang into action, fighting off the minions and driving them from his humorous home. Now as a Skylander, Funny Bone delivers his own punch line—to evil!

I HAVE A BONE TO PICK!

KAOS

Before becoming the archenemy of the Skylanders, Kaos was sent to the finest evil school of magical villainy, as were many in his long and twisted family history. It was here that Kaos met Glumshanks, who was persuaded by Kaos to become his evil servant with the promise of career growth. But soon after, they were expelled when Kaos appeared as a giant floating head at a school assembly and ate the gymnasium. With the long-suffering and still-unpromoted Glumshanks at his side, Kaos continues to come up with plan after plan to take over Skylands—some say to fulfill his ambition to become Skylands' "ultimate evil overlord," though others think that he's still trying to impress his immensely powerful and overbearing mother—herself a Dark Portal Master. All agree, however, that Kaos should never be underestimated.

BEHOLD! IT IS I, KAOS! AND AS YOU CAN SEE, I AM AWESOME!

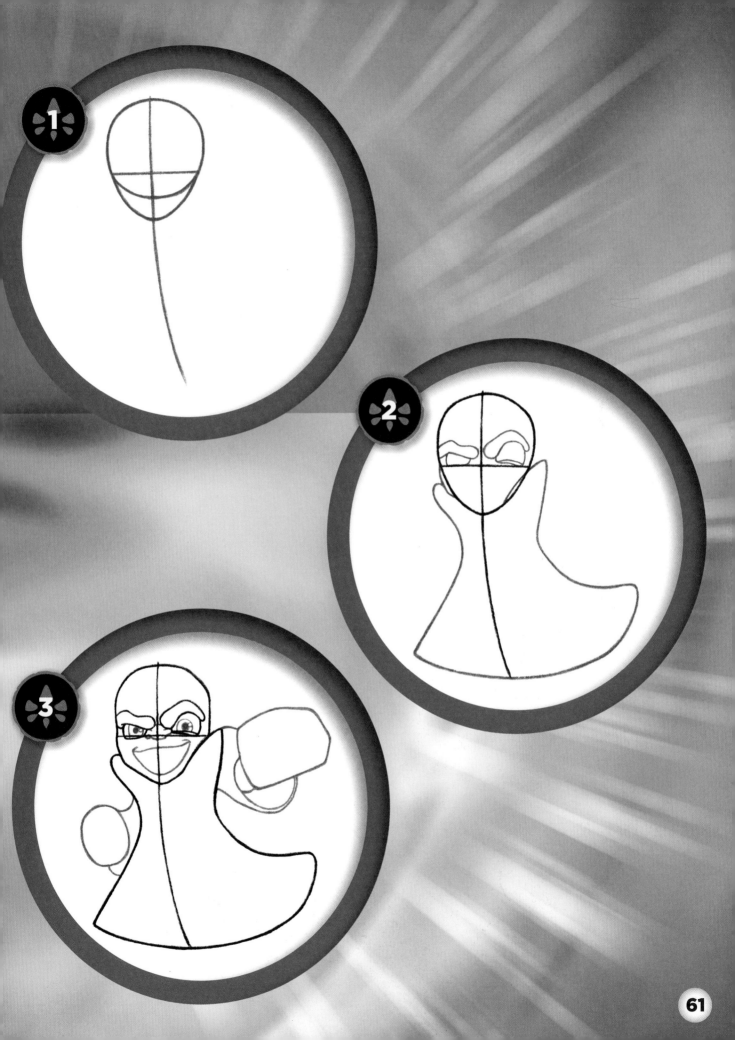

Thank you for your dedication to the Skylanders and everything they stand for. By now, you're able to draw a mighty fighting team. The Skylanders stick together, exploring the mysterious world of Skylands, collecting treasures along the way, and battling heroically when necessary. Keep practicing your drawing skills, just as the Skylanders keep practicing their unique abilities, making Skylands a safer place every day.

NOW TAKE WHAT YOU HAVE LEARNED AND TRY TO DRAW SOME OF THESE OTHER SKYLANDERS.